HOW
TO BE A
LADY

How
TO BE A
Lady

C A N D A C E
S I M P S O N - G I L E S

Thomas Nelson
Since 1798

NASHVILLE   DALLAS   MEXICO CITY   RIO DE JANEIRO   BEIJING

To my mother, Margie Smith, who taught
me that being a lady was one of the most
important parts of being a woman.

Published in Nashville, Tennessee, by Thomas Nelson. Thomas
Nelson is a trademark of Thomas Nelson, Inc.

Thomas Nelson, Inc. titles may be purchased in bulk for
educational, business, fund-raising, or sales promotional use.
For information, please e-mail SpecialMarkets@ThomasNelson.com.

Library of Congress Cataloging-in-Publication Data

Simpson-Giles, Candace, 1953–
    How to be a lady / by Candace Simpson-Giles.
        p. cm.
    ISBN: 978-1-5585-3939-6 (hardcover)
    ISBN: 978-1-4016-0185-0 (SE)
    1. Etiquette for women. I. Title.
    BJ1856 .S56 2001
    395.1'44--dc21
2001004337

Printed in the United States of America
10 11 WOR 25 24 23

CONTENTS

ACKNOWLEDGMENTS

My heartfelt gratitude goes to all who have championed and cheered with great enthusiasm as this book was birthed. You were the ones who believed that it does matter that this book is written so as to show others how to live life with grace, selflessness and great style. To all the men and women who have given me wise counsel and words of encouragement, I am grateful that I have you in my corner. Your footprints are forever within this book of guidance and inspiration on how to be a lady in life.

Thank you.

INTRODUCTION

Being a woman does not automatically make one a lady. The term lady has evolved to mean many new and different things over the past 100 years. Manners, attitudes, appropriate dress, and social mores have changed so dramatically that our grandmother's definition of being a lady hardly resembles today's expectations.

The rapid evolution of the modern woman over the last century has brought with it both confusion and fulfillment. Women have stepped back and asked themselves just exactly how to properly handle their new status and situations that arise in their professional careers and active personal lives. White gloves and hats are not as much a part of our dress standard as they were for the women of earlier generations, nor does a woman find that she has to have a male escort to attend functions.

A lady by today's definition knows that educating herself in every way possible, from higher education to the common sense manners, empowers her to become a woman of accomplishment and poise. She knows that it is not the dress size she wears or the money she possesses that brings her satisfaction in life. A lady knows that beauty and wealth can be fleeting, but her inner character is the measure by which others will ultimately judge her as a person. Her courtesies, the high esteem in which she holds herself and others, and her sincere words of praise and thoughtfulness will reflect her strong values and place her ahead in the minds and hearts of those who know her. Being thought of as a "lady" may be the one of the highest compliments a woman can receive in life.

Chapter One

A LADY EXPERIENCES REAL LIFE

When a lady is asked to be a bridesmaid, she accepts the request as an honor. If she does not particularly like the dress, she keeps this to herself.

————

A lady doesn't ask dating couples when they are getting married. Likewise, she doesn't ask married couples when or if they are planning to have children.

————

A lady never compliments one person when she is in a group setting. She chooses a moment when the two of them are alone to offer her compliment.

————

A lady knows how to prioritize her
life in order to make herself available to
family, friends, career, and other
important considerations in her life. She
also knows when she is feeling stretched
too thin and how to pull back
and sort out her priorities.

———

A lady respects other people's time
whether at the office or at home.

———

A lady never asks friends who are
professionals, such as lawyers or doctors,
for free advice in their area of specialty.
She makes an appointment to see
them at their office and fully expects
to pay for the services they provide.
Should the friends offer their services
for free or for a reduced cost,
she accepts their gesture graciously.

———

A LADY ATTENDS THE THEATER

Whether attending the theater on a date or with friends, a lady makes every possible effort to be on time for the performance. Not doing so shows a lack of respect for both the performers and fellow audience members.

If she should arrive late, a lady follows the instructions of the ushers. She realizes her tardiness may result in waiting to be seated during a break in the performance. When that break arrives, she goes to her seat as quickly and quietly as possible.

Because a lady is considerate of others around her, she does not talk during the performance. Likewise, if she must bring her cell phone with her, she turns it off before entering the theater. A well-prepared lady has a cough drop in her purse, whether for herself or the person with whom she attends the performance and, when allowed, a bottle of water. If a lady finds herself surprised by an uncontrollable coughing jag, she leaves the theater both for her own good and for the good of others.

If a lady finds herself in the company of someone who is embarrassing her, she may ask to be taken home. Should her friend refuse, a lady may feel free to leave, even if that means calling a cab or asking another friend for a ride home.

A lady is prepared when she walks up to an ATM machine or is in the drive-thru lane at a bank. If she isn't prepared, she offers to let the person in line behind her go first while she fills out her deposit slip.

At the laundromat, a lady never takes another person's laundry out of the washer or the dryer, no matter how long she has been waiting. If she is in a hurry, she asks for the attendant's assistance. If there is no attendant, she chooses another laundromat.

———

If a lady must excuse herself from the dinner table, she simply says, "Excuse me." No further explanation is necessary.

———

A lady returns any item she borrows in a timely manner and in the same condition she received it.

———

A lady never makes a date out of desperation.

———

A lady doesn't discuss her breakups
with others.

———

A lady never gives the impression she is
on the rebound.

———

A lady never points out the
imperfections of her mate to others.

———

A lady is always on her toes; she realizes
that every encounter makes lasting
impressions.

———

When walking her dog, a lady always
cleans up after her pet.

———

A lady learns how she looks best when
being photographed.

———

A LADY ATTENDS A FUNERAL

A lady recognizes that a funeral is a time for paying her respects. She wears a conservative dark suit or dress. If there is a wake, a reception, or a visitation with the deceased's family, she arrives on time and waits quietly in the receiving line. She keeps her thoughts simple and sincere with remarks such as "I am so sorry for the loss of your son. He was a good friend to me and I will miss him and his wonderful spirit."

Conversation with others during the service should be limited, and a lady sits where the ushers (if there are any) instruct her. A lady always signs the guest book.

A lady may attend the funeral or service of anyone she has known personally or professionally, at least if they have been on speaking terms. If the deceased person has shown her a particular kindness—especially

if she has ever been entertained in the
deceased person's home—a lady makes a
point to show her respect.

A lady leaves her cell phone at home
if at all possible when she is enjoying
a night out on the town.

———

A lady always turns off her cell phone
or beeper when she is attending any
type of performance, religious service,
or business meeting. If she is on call
or expecting an important call,
she puts her phone on vibrate.

———

A lady never points out another's
bad manners.

———

If a lady arrives late for a performance of any type, she waits until there is an appropriate pause and then very quietly slips into her seat.

―――――

If a lady arrives late for a church service or a funeral, she waits until there is an appropriate pause and then very quietly slips into the first available seat in the back of the sanctuary.

―――――

A lady makes every effort not to be late.

―――――

A lady stays away from public gatherings (and even work) if she feels that she is contagious or has a fever.

―――――

A lady knows how to make others feel at ease.

―――――

A Lady Experiences Real Life

A LADY GOES THROUGH A CHECKOUT LINE

A lady is prone to run into many friends and acquaintances on her trips to the grocery store. And while she gladly listens to stories about friends' vacations and newborn babies in front of the fresh pasta (as long as she is not blocking the accessibility of others), once a lady arrives at the checkout line, she is all business.

A lady does not needlessly hold up the checkout line. At the register she has her method of payment ready with coupons in hand. She never goes through the express line when she has too many items. If another shopper engages her in conversation, a lady does not hold up those waiting behind her or the cashier. A lady knows that it is her job to make the checkout lines of life move along.

Whenever possible, a lady excuses herself when she has a sneezing attack or a profusely runny nose.

———

A lady doesn't talk during a performance, a sermon, or a lecture.

———

If a lady arrives at a door first, she opens it for the person entering behind her.

———

A lady is gracious and thankful for any gesture of common courtesy directed toward her.

———

At a concert or any other musical performance, a lady does not applaud until the end of a complete musical number. If she is unsure, she follows the lead of others in the audience.

———

If a lady has left a message for another person, she does not leave badgering follow-up calls, especially if no deadline is involved.

————

A lady knows that the gym is her opportunity to get in shape. She should be focused on her workout and dressed appropriately so she is not a distraction to others or even to herself as she jogs or does aerobic movements. A lady is careful to wear clothes that support her bust line and wears tights or shorts that are complimentary to her figure and functional at the same time. She doesn't use the gym for getting dates or catching up on the latest gossip. A lady knows that if she is serious at the gym, it will pay off.

————

A lady should always be a good neighbor and offer help when she sees it is needed.

————

A LADY TAKES AN AIRPLANE FLIGHT

Almost invariably, the passengers on an airplane have been brought together by a mix of chance and necessity. A lady understands that, in such situations, it is important for everyone to abide by the rules.

She brings on board only the amount of luggage that is permitted. She is careful when she stows it overhead to prevent injury to her fellow passengers and to herself. If a bag or parcel is small enough, she stows it under the seat in front of her. She does not intrude on space that is allotted for another passenger's use. She sits in the seat that is assigned to her. If she has sat in the wrong seat and is asked to move, she does not argue about it.

She gets up and finds the place to which she has been assigned. On the other hand, she feels no obligation to give up her rightful seat to another person.

If it is at all possible, a lady stays in her seat throughout the entire flight. A trip to the rest room is almost the only excuse to do otherwise. On extremely long flights a lady does not hesitate to leave her seat for a short time to stretch her legs. When she must leave her seat, a lady excuses herself as unobtrusively as possible, making sure not to step on other passengers' feet.

An airplane flight is one of the few instances in life when it is entirely appropriate for two people to be together for several hours and never speak at all. They may begin the flight as strangers and end it the same way, without anyone having reason to feel neglected or insulted.

A lady graciously accepts a compliment. She does not downgrade herself as if she did not deserve the admiration from the other person or persons. She simply responds with, "Thank you."

———

A lady never eats her lunch while she is behind the wheel of a car.

———

A lady knows how to behave in other people's churches. If the congregation stands, she stands. She does not, however, need to cross herself, bow, or kneel.

———

A lady does not use her car horn indiscriminately. On the other hand, she is not sheepish about giving an occasional honk to avert disaster.

———

A lady uses her turn signals.

———

A lady doesn't put her makeup
on while driving a car.

———

A lady parks her car carefully. She does
not bang her car door into the vehicle
next to her. If she scratches another car,
she leaves a note.

———

A lady does not telephone someone's
home at a terribly early or extremely late
hour unless it is an emergency. She is
also careful to try to avoid making calls
to a person during what may
be a dinner hour.

———

A lady who lives in a condominium or
an apartment is mindful of her neighbors
and keeps the volume of her television
set and stereo at a level she knows
will not disturb others.

———

A lady never takes her pets to other people's homes, unless she is specifically urged to do so.

———

A lady does not feel obligated to invite other people's pets to her home.

———

A lady doesn't encourage another person's dog to bark nor does she tease it.

———

A lady does not touch other people's children unless she is invited to do so. Neither does she overexcite them.

———

To establish a friendly relationship with the hotel concierge, a lady asks the concierge for some necessary service, one that is important enough to justify a substantial tip.

———

If a bellhop offers to assist a lady in hailing a cab, a lady may accept the offer, but understands that a tip is implied.

———

When a lady recognizes friends and acquaintances at other tables in a restaurant, she feels free to greet them, but only in the least intrusive way possible. She may stop by their table to greet them cordially, but she does not interrupt their dinner or their conservation for long.

———

When a lady makes her way down a row in a crowded theater, she faces the people who are already in their seats. A lady never forces others to stare at her backside.

———

A lady always says something nice about someone or just doesn't speak of him or her at all. A lady lets people form their own opinions of others.

———

A lady doesn't kiss and tell.

————

When a lady agrees to be a bridesmaid, she understands that she will be asked to pitch in on some gifts.

————

A lady is quick to compliment the good manners of another lady's children.

————

When a lady is in the presence of a sneezing person, she offers a quick "Bless you" or, at the very least, a secular but caring "Gesundheit!"

————

If a lady lives in an upstairs apartment or condominium, she remembers that high heels make a ghastly chatter upon hardwood floors.

————

When a lady vacates a house or
apartment where she has been living,
she leaves it clean.

———

Chapter 2

A LADY GETS DRESSED

When a lady is unsure of how to dress for a particular occasion, she asks her host.

———

A lady does not wear clothes so revealing that they embarrass others.

———

A lady thinks about who will be attending an event before she chooses her wardrobe.

———

A lady has her heels resoled and the taps replaced when needed.

———

A lady makes sure her shoes are
appropriately polished.

———

A lady knows what color shoes
to wear with her outfit.

———

A lady does not wear shoes that clash
with the rest of her outfit.

———

A lady wears a camisole if her blouse
or dress is sheer enough to reveal
the details of her bra.

———

A lady builds her wardrobe on a
foundation of well-made clothes that will
not be out of style after one season and
will endure repeated cleaning and wear.

———

A LADY AND HER PURSE

In our style-conscious society of designer labels gracing every article that a woman wears or carries on her person, we must address the appropriate styles and situations in which it is necessary for a woman to carry a purse or briefcase. The usefulness, size, and function of these important carry-alls have run the gamut over the years of increasing change in women's roles in the workplace and lifestyle traverses. Some feel that they can't go anywhere without one. And some take everything but the kitchen sink in them, creating a possible need for chiropractic adjustments later in life when their shoulder gives out. Then there are the free-spirited women who consider any size purse a great deal of hassle and find them an encumbrance. All in all, there are some rules of thumb that one might consider when looking at the best size for the occasion.

A lady does not carry a bag that could be considered a "lethal weapon" on an airplane or other closely crowded environment as she walks past others. Maneuvering down an aisle with a huge bulky purse that weighs ten or fifteen pounds can slow down the journey and also might injure a seated individual by hitting him or her in the head as she passes by.

Make sure the purse fits the occasion. A small beaded bag is wonderful for weddings or formal events at which a lady is wearing elegant attire.

A moderately sized leather bag is a complementary look for a business cocktail event or lunch meeting. A bulky purse will only be hard to maneuver in a crowd or in a restaurant. (Note: A lady does not place her purse where a waiter might trip over it while serving others at her table.)When calling on a business client, it can be awkward to have both a briefcase *and* a purse to carry on the appointment. Soft-sided briefcases have now been conveniently designed with many compartments and pockets that can serve the purpose of concealing lipstick, credit cards and other small necessities that a woman might need during her business visit.

While traveling on vacation, large purses can be appropriate for making sure that a lady has all her essentials. Transferring a few things to a smaller bag upon entering restaurants or other places for a short time might be the best alternative to carrying such a heavy load on her shoulder during her travels. Some of us call them "date" purses. A little more dainty for the moment, but allowing that she has all her personal needs in a larger purse kept in the car or back at the hotel.

A purse can reflect a lady's personality and attitude for the occasion. It can be as important as the right jewelry some fashion stylists assert. Carrying one in good taste that befits the dress and the social setting, gives a lady that special confidence that she enjoys when she knows she looks her best.

A lady knows that her posture is as important as any article of clothing on her back.

———

A lady does not dump the contents of her purse on the table for all to see.

———

A lady does not buy clothes a size too small in hopes she will one day be able to wear them.

———

A lady does not wear strappy sandals and airy open-toed shoes when working in a conservative business environment.

———

A lady is careful about the jewelry she wears. She should prefer to have someone looking her in the eye instead of watching her earrings swing back and forth during an animated conversation.

———

A lady gets a pedicure in preparation for the warm weather months.

———

A lady is mindful of her appearance at all times.

———

If a lady chooses to wear nail polish, she makes sure it is not chipped.

———

A lady never paints her nails in public.

———

A lady does not wear linen before Easter nor after Labor Day.

———

A lady doesn't wear white shoes before Easter nor after Labor Day.

———

A lady who colors her hair knows when her roots are showing and makes an appointment with her stylist.

———

If a lady expects her legs to be seen, she either shaves her legs or wears hose.

———

A LADY GOES ON A DATE

Over the course of her lifetime, a lady will be presented with many opportunities for dating. And whether her date takes her to an elegant restaurant or a rock concert, a lady knows how to handle herself in every social situation.

Because a lady knows herself, she knows how long it will take her to get ready. And for that reason, a lady is always ready when her date arrives. She knows that reservations, theater curtains, and a lot of men will not wait because she can't decide what to wear. If knowing how to dress for an evening is the problem, the lady asks her date beforehand. Should it be a "first date," a lady should feel free to ask what kind of restaurant they are going to, not only so that she will know how to dress, but also because it gives her the opportunity to let her date know if the restaurant isn't her cup of tea or about any food allergies she may have.

At a restaurant a lady should by all means order what she likes to eat. A lady does not order a small dinner salad when she really wants the pasta. But at the same time, a lady does not order the most expensive item on the menu.

It's a fact of life that not everyone has that special chemistry. Occasionally a lady finds her date is someone with whom she has nothing in common. Only in the case of a potential health risk does a lady complain about the restaurant. But if is it only a matter of boredom, a lady finishes the evening and thanks him. Under no circumstances does a lady feign a headache or suddenly remember a previous engagement.

Throughout the evening (for example when a gentleman pulls her chair out for her or as they are leaving the restaurant),

and especially at the end of the evening, a
lady thanks her date for inviting her to
spend an evening with him.

A lady realizes that the purse she carries
(if she carries one at all) makes a
statement about her.

———

A lady never adjusts her bra or bustline
within view of other people. She also
does not let her bra straps show unless
they were meant to show.

———

A lady tips the person who shampoos
her hair at her salon.

———

A LADY AND HER LUGGAGE

Whether on an overnight business trip or a grand tour of Europe, a lady will find many occasions when she will need to pack a suitcase. Keeping in mind that there may be times when she must handle her own luggage, a lady does not pack her entire wardrobe for a weekend at a country inn. She thinks ahead and takes just enough, with maybe one extra outfit to get her through her trip.

A lady does not attempt to carry more luggage on an airplane than is allowed by the airline. If she is unsure of the number of pieces of luggage allowed, she calls and asks. If a lady is attempting to carry on a piece of luggage that may weigh more than she can comfortably lift herself, she checks it. Although oftentimes there will be a gentleman who will be happy to help a lady with her luggage, she cannot count on this.

Hotels today usually provide hair dryers, irons, and other items that a lady may think of as necessities. Before packing and lugging them around the globe, a lady calls and finds out if the hotel offers these items.

And because mistakes do happen, a lady makes sure her bags are identifiable from others and that her luggage tags are up-to-date in the event of lost luggage.

A lady donates the clothing she no longer wears to those less fortunate than she.

⎯⎯⎯⎯

A lady owns an evening bag or a small purse for special nighttime events.

⎯⎯⎯⎯

A lady never asks another lady what her outfit cost or what size it is.

———

A lady does not feel the urge to wear eight rings on one hand.

———

A lady follows the lead of her supervisor when determining how to dress.

———

A lady knows that her travel agent is a fount of knowledge when needing advice on how to dress for a vacation.

———

A lady knows whether she has the figure to wear tight clothing. She knows that just because an item of clothing comes in her size does not mean she should wear it.

———

A LADY GOES TO A WEDDING

Obviously, a lady only attends weddings to which she has been invited. If her invitation does not say "and guest," she attends alone, even if a reception follows. She arrives on time and sits on the appropriate side of the aisle (the left side if she is a friend of the bride, the right side if she is a friend of the groom; if she knows them both, she sits on the side with the greater number of empty seats). During the ceremony she stands when everyone else does, and she does not chat during the music. At the reception she speaks to the bride and groom and to their parents (no matter how many divorces are involved).

When choosing her attire for a wedding, a lady is careful not to choose anything that will upstage the bride.

A lady realizes that the bride is the star of the show and all attention should be on her.

A lady never wears white to a wedding unless it is her own. She is also mindful that the fabric she is wearing is appropriate for the season. For daytime weddings, a lady chooses a dress or a suit that is softer than her usual business attire. For an early evening wedding, a lady may choose a cocktail dress or a dressier suit. Floor length or three-quarter length dresses are appropriate for formal weddings.

A lady wears clean and fresh underwear.

A lady knows when she needs to wear a slip or a half-slip and does so.

A lady never purchases an item of clothing with the express intent of wearing it once and returning it later.

———

A lady wears hosiery to formal weddings and dinners, as well as in formal business settings.

———

A lady should never ask someone if she looks fat in something.

———

A lady knows that whenever there is a doubt about the color, black is best.

———

A lady knows that trends come and go, while true style is timeless.

———

A lady knows that false congeniality is as obvious as bad false eyelashes.

———

Even if she doesn't agree with them, a lady does not belittle anyone about wearing fur and leather. If this is an important cause in her life, she volunteers her time and her money to make changes. She does not confront or embarrass others.

———

Chapter Three

A LADY GOES TO DINNER

Unless absolutely necessary, a lady does not carry her cellular phone into a restaurant. If she must, she turns it off.

———

A lady knows when it is acceptable to eat the garnish.

———

When a lady has an unpleasant time in a restaurant, she does not badger the wait staff. She lodges her complaint with the management. Unless she is a glutton for punishment, she does not go back to that restaurant.

———

A LADY LEAVES A TIP

When a lady is dining alone or with friends and has accepted responsibility for settling the check, she also knows it is her responsibility to leave a tip for the server. A tip of 15 percent of the total bill is expected for good service. A tip of 20 percent or more is justified for superior service. Likewise, if a lady feels the service she or her party has received is inferior, she is justified in leaving 10 percent. At no time does a lady attempt to be cute by leaving a penny or a quarter as a sign of her dissatisfaction.

A lady does not discuss the amount she is tipping with her guests. That decision is between her and the server. But in addition to the monetary tip she leaves, a lady also publicly thanks her server for making her dining experience enjoyable.

Occasionally a lady finds herself in the

company of someone who is paying for a meal and leaves an inadequate tip. A lady does not say anything to make her companion feel cheap, but if it continues to be a problem, she may think twice about going to dinner again with that person.

A lady offers to split the dinner tab with a gentleman if she chooses. If he refuses, she graciously accepts his kindness and says thank you.

———

A lady knows when it is acceptable to drink through a straw.

———

When a lady has a bit of food lodged in her teeth and she cannot remove it discreetly, she excuses herself from the table to take care of the situation.

———

If a lady's meal is slow to arrive from the kitchen, and if others at the table have been served, she urges them, "Please go ahead without me." And she means it.

———

If a lady is on a diet, she does not talk about it at the table.

———

If a lady has invited a gentleman or any other friend out for dinner, it is her responsibility to make the reservation.

———

If a lady has not made a dinner reservation, she accepts the fact that she may have to wait in the bar.

———

HOW TO KNOW WHICH FORK TO USE

If the table has been set correctly, a lady has no problem knowing which fork, spoon, or knife to pick up first. When she sits down at the table, she will find her flatware and her cutlery set out in the order in which she will need it. When the first course arrives, she uses the fork that is farthest away from her plate. When she is finished with that course, she leaves her fork on her plate, and it is taken away. She proceeds in the same manner throughout the meal so that by the time dessert arrives, she will have only one fork, spoon, or knife left. If, by chance, the flatware has been arranged in the wrong order, a lady still follows this logical system. In such cases, the person setting the table has caused the confusion.

A lady does not talk with her
mouth full.

———

A lady knows to start with the fork on
the outside. If the salad fork is in the
wrong place, she does not make a scene.

———

When a lady finishes eating, she places
her knife and fork on her plate. She
never places a piece of dirty flatware
back on the table.

———

Once a lady's dinner knife has been
dirtied, she never lets it touch the
tablecloth.

———

A lady does not salt her food
before tasting it. She would never
insult the cook in that way.

———

How to Order a Bottle of Wine

Occasionally a lady will find herself hosting a dinner at which it will be her responsibility to select a bottle of wine. If she is confident doing this, a lady selects a wine she likes in her price range. If she is not confident doing this, she may feel free to ask her dinner guests or the server for suggestions.

In general, red wine is still the wine of choice to accompany red meat, pasta dishes with tomato sauces, and most heavy entrées. White wines are usually selected to accompany fish, chicken, salads, and pasta dishes with light sauces. However, the hostess may feel free to order any wine she likes.

As hostess, she will be presented the wine by the server who will show her the label. The server will then offer her the cork, so she can see that it is not too dry. Next, the server will pour a sip of wine in the lady's glass. A lady performs a quick taste test, and if the wine is to her liking, she allows the server to fill the glasses at her table.

The server will leave the white wine in a cooler at tableside and the red wine on the table. In either case, the hostess may wait for the server to return to refill empty glasses, or she may take care of that duty herself.

When a lady pours from a bottle of wine, she finishes by turning the bottle slightly upward, thus preventing drips that might stain.

How to make a dinner RESERVATION

A lady realizes that a dinner reservation is a verbal contract between her and the restaurant. She does not make a reservation unless she actually plans to use it, and if she must cancel or if the size of her party changes, she informs the restaurant as far ahead of time as possible.

A lady does not take it personally if a restaurant is unable to seat her party at the time she requests. If she is unable to accept a reservation at an earlier or later hour, a lady asks for a recommendation of another establishment.

If her party has special requirements—seating in a smoking or nonsmoking area, for example—a lady makes those requests when she reserves the table.

If a hostess, a manager, or a maître d' has been particularly helpful in arranging a

lady's reservation, she gladly acknowledges
that service with a tip. However, she
presents that tip as unostentatiously as
possible, perhaps slipping it into the
hostess's palm in the midst of a parting
handshake.

If a lady does not know the established
dress code of a restaurant at which she is
planning to dine, she calls ahead. If she
is the one extending an invitation to
others, she lets them know as well.

When a lady chooses not to drink
wine, she feels perfectly confident
in telling the waiter, "No thank
you. I'll just have some water
(or some iced tea or soda)."

At a cocktail party or at a seated dinner, if a lady discovers that she has put something unpleasant, or unpalatable, in her mouth, she gets rid of it in the most efficient way possible. In most cases, she simply uses her fingers or her fork. She works quickly and does not even attempt to disguise her actions behind a napkin.

————

When faced with a plate of long pasta— such as spaghetti, linguine, or fettuccine— a lady resists every temptation to chop it up with her knife and fork. Instead, she twirls a manageable mouthful around the tines of her fork and, with the help of a spoon, transfers it to her mouth.

————

A lady does not engage in a debate over politics or religion or other sensitive issues at the dinner table.

————

How to use a dinner napkin

After a lady has been seated, her first action is always to place her dinner napkin in her lap. She does not wait for the server to do so, although in some extremely fancy restaurants, that is done.

If a lady briefly leaves the table during dinner, she leaves the napkin, loosely folded, in the chair. A lady never places her napkin back on the table until she is finished with her meal and about to leave.

A lady tips graciously and as generously as the service merits.

A lady always tips the valet
parking attendant.

———

A lady never assumes that somebody
else will pick up the tab.

———

A lady never dickers over the bill.

———

If separate checks are offered in a
restaurant where a lady is dining with
friends, she asks for them.

———

A lady does not crunch her ice.

———

Although it is customary for a server to
take a lady's order first, if she isn't
prepared, she asks that others in her
party go first, even if she is the only
woman at the table.

———

Chapter Four

A LADY SAYS THE RIGHT THING

A lady does not voice strong opinions about controversial topics with total strangers or business associates who she does not know well. A lady knows that people take their opinions and issues very personally at times.

———

A lady consults the dictionary for correct spelling and definitions of words she uses in her conversations and correspondence.

———

A lady does not correct another person's grammar.

———

A lady never curses in front of others.

———

A lady knows that "please" and "thank you" are still the magic words.

———

A lady does not brag.

———

A lady does not whine.

———

A lady does not nag.

———

A lady knows how to give a compliment.

———

A lady knows how to accept a compliment by saying "Thank you."

———

How to start a
Conversation

Whether at a party, a business meeting, or formal occasion, a lady is comfortable striking up a conversation with any pleasant person she chooses. To prevent awkwardness, however, she begins with positive, noncontroversial subject matter. She says, "Isn't this a beautiful home?" or "Isn't the food just wonderful?" If the person responds cordially, she continues with a few more questions until the conversation is underway. A lady knows that she is still testing the waters. In talking with a new acquaintance she does not venture into controversial topics or voice strong politically driven opinions that may lead to an embarrassing moment.

When a lady initiates a telephone conversation, she knows it is her responsibility to end that conversation.

———

A lady never tells jokes that may embarrass other people, even if those other people are not in the room.

———

A lady does not laugh at racist, sexist, or anti-gay jokes.

———

A lady never gossips.

———

A lady always thinks before she speaks.

———

A lady knows how to make and accept an apology.

———

How to end a
Conversation

A lady realizes that every conversation
must come to an end. And she is not being
rude or inconsiderate when she attempts to
bring a chat—regardless of how charming
her friend is—to a timely close.

When a lady makes a telephone call, she
accepts the responsibility for ending that
conversation. When a conversation begins
in her office or at her work station, it is
her obligation to bring that conversation
to an end. When on the phone, a lady may
simply say, "Elizabeth, I have enjoyed our
conversation; I hope we get to talk again
soon." In person, she stands up, thanks her
guest for meeting with her, and extends
her hand for a handshake.

Even in social situations, such as a
cocktail party, a lady may end a

conversation gracefully by saying, "I have enjoyed getting to know you, Colby. Would you care to walk over to the bar along with me?" This allows the lady an opportunity to introduce Colby to other people. If Colby chooses not to accompany her to the bar, a lady says, "I am so glad we had a chance to talk."

If an apology is sincerely offered, a lady accepts it with good grace. She does not pretend that the offense never existed, but she considers it history and moves on.

———

A lady does not raise her voice when angry. It is only proper to shout at someone when he or she is in danger or about to score a touchdown.

———

How to Say, "I'm Sorry."

Although a lady always tries to be considerate of others, she is also human and occasionally makes mistakes. When that happens, a lady recognizes her shortcomings and immediately sets out to correct her wrongdoings.

When a lady apologizes, she looks the person in the eye (unless, of course, the apology is being made on the telephone) and is direct and to the point. For example, if she has had a mishap such as spilling a glass of wine on someone's rug, she may say, "Betty, I am so sorry for spilling the wine on your beautiful rug. I feel like such a klutz."

When a lady makes an apology, she means it. She says she is sorry and realizes that the apology does not downplay her mistake. Yet, she need not bring it up again and again. At the same time, a lady

never offers an insincere apology,
especially if she has done nothing wrong.

A lady uses the phrase "excuse me"
as she is moving through a crowded
room. She only says "I'm sorry" when
an apology is in order.

———

A lady excuses herself when she
is in a public place and needs to
make a call on her cell phone.

———

A lady always returns voice mail
and pages promptly.

———

A lady never mentions her monthly
period or the fact that she has cramps,
except to the closest of friends.

———

How to make a
Complaint

There are times when a lady is
perfectly justified in lodging a complaint.
If she has received poor service, if she has
been treated rudely, or if she has been the
target of an undeserved affront, she has
every right to make her displeasure
known—not only for the sake of her
bruised feelings, but also in hopes that the
unpleasantness will not occur again.

A lady knows, however, that it is useless
to make a complaint unless it is made to
the right person. For instance, if a lady has
received inferior service in a restaurant, she
does not waste her breath complaining
directly to the server, who may feel no
compulsion to change his behavior.
Instead, a lady expresses her concern to the
manager or owner of the establishment. If
she has the opportunity, she makes her

complaint in person; otherwise, she makes a telephone call or puts her concerns in writing.

When a lady makes a complaint, she gives specific reasons for her displeasure. She does not make threats. If she is served poorly at a restaurant or at any other establishment, she may choose not to take her business there again. However, if the poor service continues after she has made her complaint, she does not continue to subject herself to further unpleasantness. She takes her business elsewhere.

A lady never whispers in the presence of others. If she has something to say that can not be said in the presence of others, she waits until she and the other person are alone.

HOW TO WRITE A
SYMPATHY NOTE

It is appropriate, and even expected, for a lady to express her sympathy upon the death of someone she has known, admired, or respected. She may also wish to express her sympathy to a close friend who has lost a loved one. A lady does this in a simple yet thoughtful way. She may say, "I considered Sophie to be a close friend. I will miss her very much." To comfort a friend's loss, she may write, "I was so sorry to hear of your grandmother's passing. You are in my thoughts."

A lady never says, "Please let me know if there is anything I can do," leaving it up to the grieving person to ask for help. Instead she offers to supply a meal for the family or to pick up the mail while the person is away.

A lady knows that certain questions are too nosy to be asked, such as:

- You don't remember me do you?

- Where do I know you from?

- Are you and Bob ever going to get married?

- When are you and Bob going to have children?

———

A lady never claims to have seen a movie she hasn't seen or to have read a book about which she has only read reviews. She knows how to say, "I haven't read (or seen) that yet, but from what I hear about it, it sounds very interesting. What do you think?"

———

Chapter Five

A LADY GIVES A PARTY

A lady uses her best china or dinnerware to serve her guests. If something breaks, she is not disturbed and does not allow her guests to feel any guilt over the matter.

———

If a guest offers to bring the wine or to help in some other way with the dinner menu, a lady may either accept or decline the offer. Either way, she says, "Thank you," and means it.

———

If a guest arrives with a bottle of wine, a lady is not obligated to serve it. She accepts it as a gift to be enjoyed at her discretion.

———

How to set up a bar

A lady does not stock her bar in order to impress people. She stocks her bar with the libations people actually want to drink. For even the largest, most eclectic group, a choice of Scotch, vodka, gin, white wine, and, in the South, bourbon will suffice. What is more, her guests will find themselves much less confused.

In every case, a lady makes sure to have ample ice, and she offers a variety of mixers, not just for the pleasure of her drinking friends, but out of consideration for her teetotaling guests as well. Quality, a lady knows, is always more important than quirkiness.

A lady knows that her bar is never complete without sliced limes and lemons, a jigger, a stirrer, and a tall stack of hand-ironed, starched cotton cocktail napkins.

A lady always serves food when serving alcohol to offset its effects.

———

A lady makes it a point to know the names of the teams playing in the Super Bowl.

———

A lady makes a point to ask her dinner guests if they have any dietary restrictions she should consider before planning her menu.

———

A lady does not give surprise birthday parties or baby or bridal showers unless she is certain the honoree likes to be surprised.

———

A lady makes sugar-free sweeteners and low-calorie creamers available to her guests.

———

How to Seat a Table

If a lady entertains—whether in her home or in a public place—the moment will come when she will be expected to "seat" a table. At that moment, she, as a hostess, will be asked to decide where each of her guests will sit during the meal. A lady takes this obligation seriously, knowing that her decisions will make or break the evening. She attempts to seat compatible guests beside each another, but she never seats a couple—whether they are married, a long-standing couple, or on a first date—side by side. Her goal is to create a mix of guests who will ask one another questions, generating lively conversation.

If there is a guest of honor, that person is always given the best seat. At a banquet, for example, the honored guest is given the seat with the best view of the room. In a private home, the guest of honor is seated at the hostess's right hand or, better yet, between two particularly congenial guests.

Meanwhile, a hostess reserves for herself the least desirable seat. For instance, at a formal dinner where there are to be speeches, she takes the seat with the poorest view of the podium. Her compensatory reward comes from watching the happy faces of her handsomely entertained guests.

A lady always sets the table before her guests arrive.

———

A lady is not required to open a hostess gift in the presence of the giver unless she desires to do so.

———

About flowers and candles

A romantic dinner table really needs fresh flowers and the soft glow of candles. But the flowers should be an asset to the table, not an obstruction. A lady arranges them in a low vase or bowl, so they do not hamper eye contact between her and her guests. She shies away from overly aromatic blooms such as heavy-scented lilies, which can overpower even the strongest passion.

Candlelight makes anybody look more attractive, including the lady herself. As with flowers, candles should be positioned so that they are not an obstacle or a safety hazard. The hostess lights them just before serving the salad course, and she makes sure to snuff them out before leaving the table. (When snuffing out candles, she

cups one hand behind the flame, to
prevent hot wax from spattering across the
table and onto her guest.)

In order to make sure that her candles
can be easily lighted, a clever hostess tests
them ahead of time, letting them burn for
a few minutes so that some of the wax
slides away from the wick.

If a guest offers to help clean up after
the party, a lady may either accept
or decline the offer. However, she has
no reason to expect that such an
offer will be made.

———

A lady makes sure that her invitation,
whether it comes by telephone or by
mail, provides all the necessary
information. She gives the time, the date,
the location, and the expected attire.

———

How to set a dinner table

A lady knows how to set an elegant, if rudimentary, dinner table. The basic equipment is arranged in this manner:

WHEN SALAD IS SERVED AS A

FIRST COURSE

A. Dinner Plate	F. Coffee Spoon
B. Salad Plate	G. Dessert Spoon*
C. Salad Fork	H. Water Glass
D. Dinner Fork	I. Wine Goblet
E. Dinner Knife	J. Napkin

The Dessert Spoon can be a fork, if appropriate.

WHEN SALAD IS SERVED ALONG WITH

THE ENTRÉE

A. Dinner Plate	F. Coffee Spoon
B. Salad Plate	G. Dessert Spoon*
C. Salad Fork	H. Water Glass
D. Dinner Fork	I. Wine Goblet
E. Dinner Knife	J. Napkin

The Dessert Spoon can be a fork, if appropriate.

A lady does not hesitate to invite her guests into the kitchen as she finishes preparations for her dinner.

———

A lady is always ready before her first guest arrives. She does not answer the door in her robe half made-up.

———

If lady is still making last minute adjustments to the food, she encourages her guests to begin the first course.

———

A lady clearly lets her guests know where to park.

———

A lady lets her neighbors know when she is hosting a large number of people, especially if she has a limited amount of parking near her home.

———

How to serve dinner

Before a lady's guests arrive, she has already placed the dinner plates, flatware, and glasses on the table. Once the guests have chatted for a bit and have perhaps had a drink of some sort, she suggests that they proceed to the table. Thereafter, the procedure is as follows:

- The guests take their places.

- If a lady is serving a salad, she places the salad plates directly on the dinner plates (which have already been set).

- When the guests have finished their salads, a lady removes the salad plates. If she plans to serve the dinner plates in the kitchen, she takes them away at the same time. The salad forks should remain on the guests' plates.

- A lady either serves the dinner plates in the kitchen, or she brings the main course and its side dishes to the table, where the guests serve themselves.

- When guests have finished the main course, with second helpings if they are offered, a lady takes away the dinner plates along with the dinner forks and knives.

- Finally, a lady serves dessert. If she has not already placed the dessert forks or spoons on the table, she may bring them out along with the dessert itself. If there is coffee, she serves it now.

- If the dinner conversation continues after her guests have finished their desserts, a lady takes the empty plates away and pours more coffee. She never, never rushes her friends to leave the table after a satisfying meal.

A lady hostess realizes that her guests are her primary concern.

———

If a lady is hosting a party alone, she does not hesitate to ask a friend to help greet her guests and show them where to put their coats and purses.

———

A lady realizes it is her responsibility when her guests become inebriated. She arranges for them to be driven home by a sober friend or a cab. She takes away a guest's car keys if she has to.

———

When a guest behaves less than mannerly, a lady endures the actions of her guest, but she remembers those actions the next time she makes out her guest list.

———

Chapter Six

A LADY GOES TO A PARTY

A lady does not turn down invitations.
She never waits for something better.

———

A lady is never the last to leave a party.
Neither, if she can avoid it, is she the
first to arrive.

———

If a lady is concerned that she will be the
only "uncoupled" person at a party, she
asks the host of the party before the event.

———

A lady does not make long-distance
phone calls from other people's houses
unless she uses her phone card.

———

A lady does not dispose of her feminine hygiene products at another person's home.

————

A lady knows what RSVP means and always responds to invitations bearing that request.

————

If a lady discovers she can attend a party for which she has already declined an invitation, she calls her host and asks if she may attend.

————

Once a lady discovers that she must decline an invitation that she has already accepted, she promptly lets her host or hostess know. She gives a frank description of the reason for her change of plans and offers a sincere apology.

————

HOW TO RESPOND TO AN INVITATION

A lady wastes no time in responding to an invitation. If she sees the letters RSVP (an abbreviation for the French equivalent of "Please reply"), she is obligated to respond, either by telephone or in writing. An RSVP requires that she reply whether or not she plans to attend the event in question. If the directive is "Regrets only," she need only inform her host or hostess if she does not plan to attend.

A lady understands that it is terribly inconsiderate for her not to make her intentions known.

If a lady must decline an invitation, she gives a straightforward reason for doing so. "I have a prior engagement," "I will have guests from out of town," and "I will be away on vacation" are all perfectly acceptable explanations.

A lady does not lay down conditions for her accepting an invitation. She does not ask, "What will you be serving?" or "Who else is going to be there?" She accepts the invitation gladly and proves to herself that, because she is a lady, she can have a good time in any company, at any time.

A lady does not take a date to a party unless she is expected to do so. If her invitation is not addressed to her "and guest," she does not have the license to bring a guest.

———

Even if a lady is not having wine or a cocktail, she still raises her glass if a toast is being made. She realizes that even a glass of water, raised in the right spirit, expresses a wish for good luck.

———

If an invitation says, "Regrets only," a lady lets the host or hostess know that she does not plan to attend.

———

At a party, a lady never spends all her time talking to one person. She is always excited to meet as many people as possible, and she assumes that a great many people will enjoy meeting her, too.

———

If a lady does not see an ashtray, she does not smoke—and she does not ask if she may do so.

———

A lady uses a coaster.

———

A lady picks up any large food crumbs that she may have dropped—especially if they could cause a stain if another guest were to step on them.

———

A LADY GOES TO A PARTY

A lady is friendly to bartenders at a private party, but she is not required to leave tips for them. That is the responsibility of the host.

———

If valet parking is being provided at a party, a lady pulls into line and waits her turn. She is sure to leave the keys in the ignition.

———

If a lady has too much to drink at a party, she does not drive home. She asks another guest or the host of the party to help her find a way home.

———

A lady knows how to introduce a friend to a stranger at a party. Likewise, a lady knows how to tactfully excuse herself from the company of a party guest when she wishes to seek other companionship.

———

WHEN TO TAKE A GIFT

When a lady is invited to someone's home—for dinner, a holiday party, or for an overnight visit—she knows to take a gift. For a dinner party, she may take flowers, or a bottle of wine (unchilled, so that the host or hostess knows that it is a gift and is not intended to accompany dinner). For a holiday party, she takes a bag of coffee beans, or maybe something she has made herself, such as cookies or an ornament. If she is invited for a longer period of time—such as a weekend—a lady takes a more substantial gift, such as a coffee table book or a useful kitchen gadget.

A lady always presents her gift directly to her host or hostess. And even though she takes a gift, a lady still sends a thank-you note at the first opportunity after the event.

If a lady feels uncomfortable at a
party because of the actions of other
guests, she explains to her host that she
needs to leave and thanks the host
for a wonderful evening.

———

If a lady breaks something at a party,
she informs the host or hostess and
apologizes. She does not attempt to
pay for the item. If she wishes, she
replaces the item and presents it at
another time.

———

A lady knows when it's time
to say good night.

———

Even if a lady has brought flowers or
wine to a dinner, she still writes a
thank-you note.

———

WHEN TO SEND A
THANK-YOU NOTE

There are many reasons a lady writes a thank-you note. The acknowledgment of a gift or to express appreciation for a kind word or deed are just a couple of reasons. A lady knows that even though she brought a bottle of wine to a party she still writes a note. (The wine says, Thank you for inviting me. The note says, I had a wonderful time.)

A lady is prompt in writing thank-you notes—within ten days of receiving a gift if at all possible. Writing a note lets the giver know in a tangible way just how grateful she is for his or her generosity. The extra effort to write a thank-you note speaks volumes about a lady's courtesy.

A lady need not reply to a thank-you note.

If a lady does not wish to drink alcohol at a party, she politely refuses drinks offered to her and asks for a non-alcoholic beverage.

———

If a lady finds she has overdressed or underdressed for a party, she does not leave in a panic. She rises to the occasion and lets her personality and charm be the most noticeable thing about her. But hopefully she has learned an important lesson and will ask the host the proper attire for an event.

———

A lady always blots her lipstick well before going out so that she does not leave heavy lipstick marks on her linen napkin, wine glass, or the cheek of a friend she greets. Lipstick marks are never easy to clean and sometimes make the wrong impression.

———

In the event a lady attends a party at which someone is wearing a dress identical to hers, she simply smiles and compliments the other lady on her excellent choice in clothing

———

A lady never shows up *with* or *as* an uninvited guest to a party.

———

Chapter Seven

A LADY AND HER FRIENDS

A lady is observant of the habits and lifestyle of friends she is visiting. She does not stay up late if her host is an early riser.

———

A lady makes up her bed when she stays overnight at someone's home.

———

A lady never says or does things that make others feel small.

———

A lady never assumes that people know each other. She always makes introductions and is ready to give her own name first.

———

How to make an INTRODUCTION

Even in our increasingly casual society, a lady respects the time-honored traditions surrounding social introductions:

- A younger person is always introduced to an older person. For example, when Perry George, who is in his twenties, is introduced to Mrs. Caldwell, who is in her fifties, a lady says, "Mrs. Caldwell, I'd like you to meet Perry George." Even if a younger woman is being introduced to an older man, a lady makes sure to say the older person's name first.

- When a lady introduces a man and a woman who are of essentially the same age, she introduces the man to the woman. Thus, if her friends Angie Reese and Perry George do not know each other, a lady introduces them by saying, "Angie, this is my friend, Perry George." Then the lady turns to Perry and says, "Perry, this is Angie Reese."

- In all cases, a lady feels free to add some detail to stimulate conversation. She might, for example, say, "Mrs. Caldwell, Perry is one of my good friends from law school." Or, "Angie, you may have heard me talk about Perry. We went to the Mozart concert last week."

- A lady makes every effort to pronounce names clearly. If it is convenient, she repeats the names at some not-too-distant point in the conversation.

- Even if she is uncertain of the protocol of the moment, however, a lady always does her best to make an introduction. Even if she makes a small mistake, she has not committed the more serious mistake of being rude.

A lady uses the word *companion* when introducing two friends who live together. She realizes the term denotes a special relationship that is beyond boyfriend/girlfriend.

————

A lady knows that when faced with a question as to how to treat another person in any situation, she should remember to treat that person as she would want to be treated.

————

A lady doesn't bombard her friends with useless e-mail.

————

A lady does not assume her friends are interested in having a lengthy telephone conversation just because she wants to talk.

————

How to deal with
nondrinkers

Every lady will have friends who at times cannot, or choose not, to drink alcohol. Whatever the reason—religious belief, health, addiction, medication—a lady respects it and never pressures anyone to drink. At the same time, she does not ask why a person is not drinking—and has plenty of delicious nonalcoholic options available.

If a lady chooses not to drink alcohol, she does not impose her decision on other people. If she is offered a glass of wine, she simply says, "No, thank you, but I would love some ginger ale." She offers no further explanation.

How to shake hands

A lady may feel free to shake hands with anyone to whom she is introduced— whether at a party or in a business setting. A lady always extends her hand to a gentleman first, letting him know that she wishes to shake his hand. If she does not, then she should not expect the gentleman to extend his hand either. A gentleman has been trained to wait for a lady to extend her hand first should she wish to shake hands.

A lady offers a firm clasp. She does not offer a full-fledged up-and-down pump but a quick, gentle press. She makes sure her hands are dry and clean and looks the person in the eye as she greets him or her or says her goodbyes.

When a lady realizes that another
lady's bra strap is showing or she has
a piece of toilet paper stuck to her high
heel, she discreetly tells her about
it as soon as possible.

———

A lady is always on time. She knows
how long it takes her to get ready
and does not keep others waiting. If she
is going to be late, she phones ahead
and asks the host or hostess to begin
the meal without her.

———

A lady breaks a date only for reasons of
sickness, death, or natural disaster. If she
must cancel her plans, she does so with
as much advance notice as possible.

———

A lady allows others to finish their
thoughts and sentences.

———

A lady does not hesitate to dispel false rumors about her friends.

———

A lady lets the gentlemen friends in her life know she appreciates their behavior toward her.

———

A lady is considerate of the special needs of senior citizens and physically challenged people. For example, if she encounters a blind person who seems confused by a busy street corner, she asks, "May I help you across the street?" If the offer is accepted, the lady provides a helpful hand. If the offer is declined, she maintains her distance, keeping a watchful eye.

———

A lady opens the door for others entering a building behind her, even for men.

———

A lady does not give up her friends when she falls in love. Nor does she lose sight of who she is apart from the relationship.

———

A lady knows how to break up from relationships, leave jobs, and confront friends without losing friendships.

———

A lady knows that the ability to provide an ear to listen or a shoulder to cry on is one of the greatest gifts she can give a friend.

———

A lady is careful when loaning money to others, even close friends. If she does not feel comfortable making the loan, she does not. If she feels a legal agreement will ease her comfort level, she consults an attorney.

———

How to be a houseguest

As a guest in a private home a lady treats her host's furniture and other belongings with the greatest care, even more carefully than if they were her own.

If there are servants who provide some special service for her, or if she stays any great length of time, she shows her gratitude by leaving a thank-you tip.

In every case, a lady attempts to fit into the household routine. She rises and retires according to the household schedule. She eats what is served and does not complain. She makes her bed in the morning, and she disposes of damp towels as instructed.

Above all else, she sticks to her arrival and departure plans. When her visit is over, she checks her room to make sure she has packed all her belongings. She leaves nothing but pleasant memories behind.

A lady does not make phone calls to anyone during the dinner hour.

———

A lady is not afraid to carry breath mints. Neither is she reluctant to offer them to other people.

———

A lady never asks anyone to divulge his or her age.

———

A lady never reveals her age.

———

A lady celebrates her friends and lets them know their importance in her life.

———

A lady never begins a statement with "I don't mean to embarrass you, but..."

———

How to deal with unmarried couples

A lady may have many friends and acquaintances who live together in nontraditional relationships. If a lady decides to make these people a part of her life, she accepts them as they are, recognizing that their private lives are their business and no one else's. If she does not approve of their behavior, she does not preach to them. Instead, she associates with them as seldom as possible.

In no case does she mention their relationship when introducing them to other people. For example, a lady does not say, "This is Mary Brown, and this is her live-in boyfriend [or "her significant other" or "the father of her child"], Sam Jones." Instead, she says, "I'd like you to meet my friends Mary Brown and Sam Jones."

If the couple feels the need to provide

any further details about their living arrangement, they may do so, although in most cases they will be telling people more than they really need or want to know.

In written correspondence with Mary and Sam, a lady addresses the envelope to "Ms. Mary Brown and Mr. Sam Jones." A letter to Bob and Keith would be addressed to "Mr. Bob Grainger and Mr. Keith Harris." Kate and Helen's letter would go to "Ms. Helen Thompson and Ms. Kate Williams," listing them in alphabetical order.

A lady never asks her friends in need
what she can do for them. It is better
for a lady to respond to a need she sees
than expect her friend to come up
with a job for her.

———

A lady knows how to be a friend to
other ladies as well as to gentlemen.

———

A lady knows when saying "Thank you"
is enough and when a bouquet of
flowers is appropriate.

———

A lady knows that it is possible to offer
assistance to a gentleman without
threatening his masculinity.

———

A lady is never overly effusive when
complimenting one friend in the
presence of others.

———

How to deal with
divorced friends

A lady regrets seeing any loving
relationship break up, especially if she
considers both persons to be her friends.
However, her regret is for their pain, not for
her own. She does not take sides in their
marital strife; she does not carry tales back
and forth between the opposing camps.

If her friends are recently divorced, a
lady does not attempt to put them in
situations—a small dinner party, for
example—where they will be forced to
encounter each other. She tries to maintain
communication with both parties, but she
understands that she is now friends with
two people, not with a couple. Maintaining
these friendships may require twice as
much effort—and twice as much time.

After a reasonable amount of time has
passed, however, a lady may feel free to

include both friends in the same event, especially when a good many other people are involved. To forestall any anxiety, though, she is thoughtful enough to make sure both parties are informed ahead of time. She also makes sure that her guest list includes other single people, so that the divorced person does not feel like a fifth wheel.

A lady may say to Betsy, formerly married to Tom, "It's going to be fun, Betsy. I've invited Jim and Marcia, and Bob, Jim, Gloria, Ted and Vivian. I'm going to ask Tom too."

Because a lady's friends are well-mannered people, they would never ask her for such information ahead of time. However, a lady understands if, given the circumstances, they choose to decline her invitation. Only in such extraordinary circumstances, after all, would a well-mannered person ever decline.

Chapter Eight

A LADY GOES TO THE OFFICE

A lady never assumes she can address
her boss by her or his first name until
she has been directed to do so.

———

A lady always shows respect,
not only for her superiors, but also
for those who work for her.

———

A lady does not gossip.

———

A lady knows how to make a complaint
about her job. She does so by going to
her immediate supervisor.

———

A lady knows how to dress appropriately for the workplace. If she is to be taken seriously and respected, she must project that sense of style and posture. It starts from within and should be reflected on the outside as well. A lady should not send conflicting messages to clients and coworkers.

———

A lady avoids sexist and racist terminology.

———

A lady realizes that the office refrigerator is not the place to conduct scientific experiments. She remembers to dispose of her leftovers before they begin to smell.

———

A lady is not late for meetings.

———

THE ETIQUETTE OF THE ANSWERING MACHINE

A lady never assumes that anyone recognizes her voice on an answering machine. She speaks clearly, identifies herself, and leaves her phone number. Better yet, she speaks slowly and gives her number twice. In no case does a lady hog the tape. She leaves her message and then gets on with her life. If she needs to have a conversation, she can have one over dinner.

When a lady's phone message is not returned in a timely fashion and a deadline is involved, she calls back and, if necessary, leaves a second message. It is then the other person's responsibility to return the call.

If a lady receives a message that involves a deadline, such as a dinner invitation, she returns the message promptly.

A LADY AND HER BOSS

A lady realizes that in some situations, there is still a chain of command. While she may be on a first-name basis with her employer and they may go to the same aerobics class, she still remembers who is in charge at the office.

When in a social situation, such as having drinks after work, she accepts without resistance her boss's offer to pick up the tab. If she chooses not to accept an invitation from her boss for an after-work-hours social event, she expresses her gratitude for the invitation nonetheless.

If a lady is entertained in her boss's home, she treats her boss and her boss's spouse just as she would treat any other host or hostess. She takes a small gift if it seems appropriate and always writes a thank-you note—which is sent to their home. (She does not place the note on her boss's desk the next morning.)

If a lady receives a gift from her boss, she accepts it and expresses her gratitude. She understands that her boss does not expect a gift in return. A lady realizes that the gift acknowledges a job well done; it does not suggest an exchange between friends.

If a lady finds that breaks with other workers is only an excuse to gossip, she avoids taking breaks with her coworkers.

———

A lady does not talk excessively about business at a social event. She leaves that to regular business hours during the week.

———

A lady offers to help her coworkers who must be off work because of religious or health reasons. These favors go a long way in showing appreciation of others.

———

A lady stands when introduced to others at the office.

———

A lady makes it a point to ask for an introduction to the wife or girlfriend of a married friend or coworker. Workplace friendships are easy to begin and a lady must be careful to always keep her friendship with a married man in its proper place and context.

———

A lady speaks pleasantly and with a friendly tone when on the telephone. She does not put people on hold for extended periods of time.

———

A lady realizes that the more professionally she presents herself in the workplace, the more seriously she will be taken.

———

A lady does not smack her gum at the office.

———

A lady is careful how she acts at the yearly office party.

———

A lady writes a thank-you note after a job interview.

———

If a lady must leave her job, for whatever reason, she does so graciously. expressing appreciation to management for her learning experience with that company.

———

A lady shows up on time for work.

———

A LADY AND HER SECRETARY

A lady treats her secretary or administrative assistant, as well as every member of her staff, with the respect due a valued coworker and a fellow human being. She makes her expectations clearly known, and she readily expresses her gratitude for a job well done.

A lady is careful to keep the line clearly drawn between her personal and professional life. If her level of trust is great enough, she may ask her secretary to make her bank deposits for her in an emergency, but she does not take advantage of her assistant with tasks she simply would rather not do, like picking up her cleaning.

A lady may give her secretary a gift on special occasions—such as Secretary's Day or a birthday, but it is always wise to stick with an impersonal item. A lady does not expect a gift in return.

And regardless of the length of the relationship between boss and secretary, a lady never forgets that "please" and "thank you" are the magic words.

A lady always asks business associates if they are busy before she begins a conversation.

———

A lady does not give out business cards at personal parties or events such as weddings. If someone asks her for her card at such an outing, she fulfills his or her request.

———

A lady does not write personal correspondence on her business stationery.

———

A lady does not lie on her résumé.

————

A lady always restocks the copy
machine with paper.

————

A lady does not abuse the privileges of
her expense account.

————

When a lady entertains a business
client, even if the client is also a lady, it
is her responsibility to pick up the tab.

————

A lady always keeps business cards in
her desk and her briefcase. She keeps
them in a case and makes sure they are
clean and not bent.

————

A lady keeps her address book updated.

————

THE ETIQUETTE OF E-MAIL

A lady treats e-mail like any other written correspondence. She expresses herself clearly and concisely. She does not send lengthy sequences of short, inconsequential messages that clutter up the recipient's e-mail directory. She indicates the topic of her correspondence in the "Subject" line of her e-mail, so that the recipient can identify it quickly.

If a lady is sending a copy of her e-mail to a second correspondent, she indicates that she is sending a copy in the same way that she would use "cc:" at the bottom of a letter. She knows e-mail is never completely private since it is read on a computer screen and often in an office environment. To save embarrassment to herself and to her correspondent, she is discreet about the messages she sends.

The etiquette of the office break room

Even if a lady is not meticulous about how she behaves in her own kitchen, she maintains higher standards in the office break room or the communal kitchen. She never leaves her dirty coffee cup, her dirty dishes, or her dirty silverware in the sink. If there is no dishwasher, she washes her own dishes. She also dries them and puts them away.

If she takes the last of stocked items (paper towels, soda, or ice) she refills them. Likewise, if she takes the last cup of coffee, she makes a fresh pot.

She does not leave her leftovers in the office refrigerator for an excessively long time. And she never assumes that she has an automatic right to sample anything left in the refrigerator by a fellow employee.

At the office, as at home, a lady always refills the ice trays.

———

A lady shares her home phone number only with those business associates who really need it. She does not give out the home phone numbers of people who work with her.

———

When a lady discovers she needs to use the rest room, she leaves the meeting quietly. She does not need to announce where she is going.

———

A lady delivers messages she takes accurately and timely.

———

A lady does not barge into another person's office, even if the door has been left open.

———

A Lady Goes to the Office

A lady may choose to carry work home from the office or devote more time to her job than others do. She does not, however, assume that her fellow employees will do the same.

––––––

If a lady is in the position to supervise the work of other people in her office, she does not attempt to dictate. Instead, she directs.

––––––

A lady knows that sick children are more important than a deadline at the office.

––––––

A lady does not miss deadlines.

––––––

When a lady recognizes an outstanding contribution of a coworker, she not only expresses her feelings with the coworker but also with her boss.

––––––

A lady remains composed at the office. Should she feel herself losing composure, whether losing her temper or on the verge of tears, she calmly excuses herself.

———

Chapter Nine

A LADY TAKES CARE OF HERSELF

A lady sees her doctors on a regular basis, especially her gynecologist.

———

A lady knows that monthly breast self-exams are smart and life-saving no mater what age she is. She reports any irregularities to her doctor. Prevention and early detection are the best ways to beat breast cancer.

———

A lady never leaves discarded feminine hygiene products in an open wastebasket at someone else's home or at the office. She always properly wraps these items and discreetly disposes of them.

———

A lady knows how to defend herself
and takes a self-defense course if
she chooses.

———

A lady does not hug other people
after she has been working out or
running unless she explains what she
has been doing and her friend insists
on a hug anyway.

———

When a lady senses that she is not in a
safe place, she leaves as calmly and
quickly as possible.

———

When faced with life's minor setbacks,
a lady does not act like a victim.

———

When life deals bad breaks,
a lady rises above them.

———

SMOKING

A lady knows that smoking is harmful to her health. If she chooses to smoke, a lady is considerate about other people's air space. A lady never smokes when pregnant, knowing that it is harmful— possibly deadly—to her baby and may cause complications in her pregnancy, such as low birth weight or premature deliveries.

A lady does not smoke around children nor does she smoke around expectant mothers. She knows that secondhand smoke is harmful to children in and outside the womb, causing asthmatic symptoms.

A lady knows the risk that smoking has on her reproductive health and weighs the risks and harmful effects before deciding to take up such a habit.

A Lady and Breast Cancer

Breast cancer can occur at any age, young or old, but a lady knows it is smart to check monthly for signs of a lump, tenderness, or discoloration on any part of her breasts. She is proactive by making an appointment with her doctor if she notices an unexplained change. She knows that an early diagnosis of breast cancer can save her life as she faces the challenge of keeping herself well with a healthy body.

A lady is not ashamed to ask for the sexual history of a man with whom she may become intimate.

———

A lady does not lead men on.

———

A lady is never afraid to go to the
proper authority figures to report
inappropriate physical or sexual abuse.

———

A lady never gives her telephone
number to a stranger over the Internet. If
she wishes to meet someone she has
chatted with, she arranges to meet him
or her in a safe place.

———

A lady expects the men in her life
to understand the meaning of the word
"no." Otherwise, she simply does not
make them a part of her life.

———

A lady has a circle of friends and family
members to whom she goes for advice
and counsel.

———

A LADY TAKES CARE OF HERSELF

A LADY AND THE
GYNECOLOGIST

A lady makes yearly appointments with her doctor or gynecologist to insure that she stays healthy and aware of any problems. She is smart to make a Pap smear part of her regular checkup because she knows that her body can go through strong hormonal changes that can lead to emotional and physical distress.

A lady makes an appointment with her gynecologist if she experiences any change in her menstrual cycle—heavier or longer bleeding time, spotting in between monthly periods, or pain that is prolonged and unusual. She knows that early detection of reproductive problems can lead to cures and safeguard her from infertility.

A lady is always careful to properly wrap and dispose of feminine products during her menstrual period. She never leaves them in an open wastebasket at work or at someone's home.

It is often tempting to discuss the discomfort of monthly cramps or other ailments due to a lady's menstrual cycle. But a lady is never tempted to discuss this personal subject in the presence of acquaintances or where the conversation might be overheard by strangers. She knows the value of privacy in this matter.

A lady never gets behind the wheel of her car if she has had too much to drink.

———

A lady is cautious not to put herself in harmful situations that could endanger her safety or compromise her own personal value system for living.

———

If a lady doesn't see well, she wears her glasses or her contact lenses. She doesn't let vanity stand in her way of seeing all life has to offer—including traffic signals and turn signals on the road.

———

A lady does not just order a salad at a restaurant when she is on a date if she really wants a hamburger. She realizes the men who would not want her because she has an appetite are not worth the trouble.

———

A LADY PROTECTS HERSELF

In a world where everyone's personal safety has been challenged—in schools, the workplace, parking lots and even while pumping gas at a busy service station—a lady equips herself with knowledge and skills necessary for protecting herself if threatened. She reads articles, attends programs, or takes self-defense courses to prepare herself should there ever be an unexpected assault or attack.

A lady knows that her posture and confident appearance can help deter an attacker from choosing her as his next victim. She walks with her shoulders back and her head and chin high, giving her an air of power and self-assurance to an outside observer. A lady knows that her confident body language makes her appear to be less vulnerable or a passive victim.

When a lady senses she is not in a safe

place or if a person gives her cause to doubt that he or she is safe to be around, she leaves calmly and quickly. She does not give off the sense of fear to the person she feels unsafe around. This might make him or her react with a threatening manner or action.

When a lady's car breaks down on the highway, she does not attempt to flag down a passing motorist. Instead, she uses her cell phone, or waits for a law enforcement officer to arrive.

A lady stands up for herself and is never a doormat.

A LADY AND HER SURROUNDINGS

- Regardless of how prepared she is for possible attacks, a lady should try to avoid at all costs situations and places that may put her at risk.

- When pumping gas, a lady makes sure that no one enters the car from the passenger side.

- A lady looks underneath the car and in the back seat before entering.

- A lady is careful not to park next to a van in a parking lot. Women have been abducted from parking lots when snatched by someone jumping from vans and pulling them back into the vehicle.

- A lady is careful to always keep the doors to her home and her automobile locked.

- A lady does not walk through a parking lot alone if possible. She is aware of the people around her and in particular anyone who may be following her.

- Ladies on cell phones and fumbling in their purses are already distracted and easier targets for robbery and abduction.

- Women are less likely to become a target if they are carrying an umbrella or another sharp object that can be used from a distance.

- A lady knows that the groin area on a man is his most vulnerable spot. Go for it and knee an attacker. He will be rendered helpless and you can escape.

- Do not be passive. Yell! Scream! Kick!

A lady knows that she is at her best when she is in good health. And for that reason, she doesn't ignore her health.

———

A lady realizes that a tan is not worth the risk of skin cancer. She uses sun block when she goes out in the sun. A lady knows there are many products on the market today that will give her the appearance of a tan without the danger.

———

Chapter Ten

A LADY AND EXTREME ETIQUETTE

WHITE HOUSE

If a lady is invited to the White House, she must take advantage of this opportunity and go with much excitement. Depending on the formality of the invitation (engraved on heavy paper, complete with the presidential seal), a lady should reply with a written formal note of acceptance. Should she receive a less formal invitation in the form of a phone call or a letter from the First Lady's assistant or the President's secretary, the lady should respond in the manner in which the invitation was issued. A formal invitation should be responded to with formal stationery, whereas a phone call or personal invitation may be responded to with personal stationery.

When visiting the White House, a lady dresses in her best suit or dress for daytime events or evening wear if attending an event at night.

She is always cautious to be moderate with her alcohol and she does not smoke at any time on the White House premises.

Realizing that the schedules of the president and First Lady are quite full to say the least, a lady accepts whatever time she is scheduled and is prepared to say her good-byes at the allotted time. If she is fortunate enough to be asked to have her photograph taken with either member of the first family, she accepts and stands where she is directed to, even if that is not her "best side."

And even though it is the White House, a lady promptly sends a thank-you note to express her appreciation for the time she was fortunate to spend with our country's leaders.

WHEN YOU MEET THE PRESIDENT

When a lady is in the receiving line to meet the President, she goes behind her male companion if she is being accompanied. She addresses the president as "Mr. or Madame President" as the case may be or "Sir" or "Ma'am".

The president's spouse is greeted by his or her married name as in "Mrs. Reagan" or "Mr. Reagan."

No one in the room sits until the president and his or her spouse sit down.

A lady waits for the president to initiate a handshake and any passing conversation. Even if she does not agree with a recent action this president has taken, she does not use this time to express her displeasure.

An Audience with The Pope

When a lady visits Rome, the highlight of her visit would be to obtain an audience with the pope. Whether she is Catholic or non-Catholic, a lady will need great connections to gain an audience. Her request must be arranged through prominent Catholic laymen or a member of the Catholic clergy. When her request is granted, she will receive a ticket for an audience at a specific time at the Vatican. The concierge can give her further information she may need about the procedures.

A lady must be careful to dress in a black or dark everyday dress that has sleeves, a conservative neckline, and a skirt length that is not too short. Her hair must be covered. Bare legs are not acceptable. In other words, hosiery of some kind is necessary or dress pants are permitted.

Everyone must stand as the pope enters and leaves the audience chamber. The service will consist of a brief sermon by the pope followed by a blessing. Even non-Catholics are expected to kneel and stand along with the rest of the congregation. However, they need not cross themselves. If there is time, the pope may greet the visitors individually. The pope is referred to as Your Holiness.

A lady knows that the Vatican is not only the headquarters for the Catholic Church, but it is also one of the most famous tourist attractions in the world. For that reason, a lady makes sure to allow plenty of time to arrive at the Vatican well before her audience with the Pope.

MEETING OTHER
PUBLIC FIGURES

A lady might find herself with the opportunity to meet someone of celebrity or fame during her lifetime and she should be well prepared to keep her respect and adulation in check. Whether it's dining out, charity functions, or business conventions, she might find herself face to face with a well-known sports, political, or entertainment figure.

No matter how excited she is to meet this person, she should neither force a conversation upon him or her nor ask for an autograph. Celebrities so often hear the same compliments or questions and are frequently stopped for random autographs. It is best to only take an autograph if that is part of the celebrity's activity at the event and pictures are readily being made available for guests to receive an autograph–such as a sports banquet or sports convention.

One must never interrupt a celebrity while he or she is speaking with someone else and especially if the celebrity is dining with others. If a lady does find herself in an opportune moment to speak with this person she should keep it brief and when finished, she says, "I have enjoyed meeting and talking with you. Thank you for your time."

A lady does not gush about her admiration of the public figure and never lets them know she has been a fan since she was a little girl (even if she has.) Likewise a lady never tells a celebrity that they look younger, thinner, better (pick one) than they do on television (again, even if they do.)

MEETING ROYALTY

A lady perhaps has dreamed of meeting royalty or even envisioned herself as becoming a princess one day. Meeting or encountering royalty will encompass some different etiquette rules that don't apply in the United States. A lady should be prepared for that special moment by being informed of a few important courtesies.

If a lady is in line to meet anyone of royalty, she should never initiate any conversation. If spoken to, then she may reply with a simple, "So nice to meet you Ma'am (or Sir)". If a hand is extended toward her, then she may extend her hand for a polite shake. If the person of royalty asks questions of the lady, then she may answer them briefly and articulately. She will let the person of royalty bring the conversation to a close.

Should a lady have the opportunity to meet the Queen of England, she may either choose to curtsey (as is the tradition with British women), or she may just shake hands if a hand is extended toward her. Otherwise, when it comes to greeting royalty, the policy is hands-off.

If a lady knows there is a chance she may have an encounter with a member of the royal family she does her homework and learns something about the family's history so that she knows enough about their home and their country to carry on a polite conversation.

OTHER FORMS OF ADDRESS
FOR DIGNITARIES

THE VICE PRESIDENT

Mr. (Madame) Vice President or

Sir (Madame)

A UNITED STATES SENATOR

Senator _____

A MEMBER OF THE HOUSE OF

REPRESENTATIVES

Representative _____

GOVERNOR OF A STATE

Governor _____

AN EPISCOPAL OR ROMAN CATHOLIC BISHOP

Bishop _____

A ROMAN CATHOLIC ARCHBISHOP

Your Excellency

A RABBI

Rabbi _____

A MEMBER OF THE PROTESTANT CLERGY

Mr. _____, Mrs. _____,

Ms. _____, or Dr. _____

Extremely formal moments at the dinner table

How to Use a Finger Bowl

Finger bowls can be a lifesaver when eating messy seafood such as crab legs or lobster or other food eaten with your hands. A lady might be presented with a finger bowl while dining at a formal dinner which could be placed in the dessert plate on a doily. This is usually a small glass bowl filled three quarters with water and perhaps a lemon or flower floating in the bowl of water. A lady should only dip her fingertips in the bowl of water and then dry them with her napkin. Should a lady's finger bowl be placed on her dessert plate, she should move the bowl and doily to the upper left corner of her place setting and then move her fork and spoon to the right and left of her dessert plate.

It's Sorbet....and It's the Middle of Dinner!

Ice cream arriving in the middle of dinner might leave some confused about what to do . . . but not an informed lady. She simply takes a few bites to clear her palate from the heavy taste of the entrée and leaves the rest of the sorbet to be taken away. This citrus or liqueur flavored sorbet in a dish is not dessert and is usually followed by a salad course. Bon Apétit!

John Bridges and Bryan Curtis created the Gentlemanners series with a simple goal in mind: to provide people with the tools to make this planet a nicer, more civilized place to live in a manner that is neither snobbish nor intimidating. We believe that the down-to-earth style sets this series of books that celebrate the mannerly way of life apart from most etiquette books on the market.

HOW TO BE A GENTLEMAN

A GENTLEMAN ENTERTAINS

AS A GENTLEMAN WOULD SAY

A GENTLEMAN GETS DRESSED UP

A GENTLEMAN AT THE TABLE

TOASTS AND TRIBUTES

HOW TO BE A LADY

AS A LADY WOULD SAY

A LADY AT THE TABLE

HOW TO RAISE A LADY

HOW TO RAISE A GENTLEMAN

Available wherever books are sold.